LORENZINO

Borgo Press Books by Alexandre Dumas

Anthony
The Barricade at Clichy
Bathilda
Caligula
The Corsican Brothers
The Count of Monte Cristo, Part One: The Betrayal of Edmond Dantès
The Count of Monte Cristo, Part Two: The Resurrection of Edmond Dantès
The Count of Monte Cristo, Part Three: The Rise of Monte Cristo
The Count of Monte Cristo, Part Four: The Revenge of Monte Cristo
A Fairy Tale (with Adolphe de Leuven and Léon Lhérie)
The Gold Thieves
The Last of the Three Musketeers; or, The Prisoner of the Bastille (Musketeers #3)
Lorenzino
The Mohican's War
Napoléon Bonaparte
Queen Margot
Richard Darlington (with Prosper Dinaux)
Sylvandire
The Three Musketeers (Musketeers #1)
The Three Musketeers—Twenty Years Later (Musketeers #2)
The Tower of Nesle (with Frédéric Gaillardet)
The Two Dianas; or, Martin Guerre (with Paul Meurice)
Urbain Grandier and the Devils of Loudon
The Venetian (with Auguste Anicet-Bourgeois)
The Whites and the Blues
The Widow's Husband; and, Porthos in Search of an Outfit
Young Louix XIV

Related Dramas:

The Queen's Necklace, by Pierre Decourcelle
The Seed of the Musketeers, by Paul de Kock & Guénée (Musketeers #5)
The San Felice, by Maurice Drack
The Son of Porthos the Musketeer, by Émile Blavet (Musketeers #4)
A Summer Night's Dream, by Adolphe de Leuven and Joseph-Bernard Rosier
The Widow's Husband; and, Porthos in Search of an Outfit: Two Dumasian Comedies, edited by Frank J. Morloc

LORENZINO

A PLAY IN FIVE ACTS

ALEXANDRE DUMAS

Translated and Adapted by Frank J. Morlock

THE BORGO PRESS
MMXII

LORENZINO

Copyright © 1999, 2012 by Frank J. Morlock

FIRST BORGO PRESS EDITION

Published by Wildside Press LLC

www.wildsidebooks.com

DEDICATION

*For Dan Woloshen,
for many years of friendship*

CONTENTS

CAST OF CHARACTERS 9
ACT I 11
ACT II 55
ACT III 117
ACT IV 141
ACT V 161
ABOUT THE AUTHOR 187

CAST OF CHARACTERS

Duke Alexander

Lorenzino

Michel

Fra Leonardo

Filippo Strozzi

Matteo

The Hungarian

Jacopo

Bernardo Corsini

Vittorio dei Pazzi

Birbante

Selvaggio Aldobrandini

Marquis of Cibo

Luisa

A Master of Arms

Familiar of the Inquisition

Monks

Soldiers

Prisoners

ACT I

Florence. The 2nd and 3rd of January 1537.

The square of Santa Maria, Florence. To the left of the spectators a wall from which hang long festoons of ivy. Above the pinnacles of the wall appear branches shorn of their leaves. Further back the convent of Santa Croce. To the right a row of houses. Before these is a well with iron ornaments. It is midnight—and the stage is lit only by candles that burn before a Madonna placed in a niche at corner of the convent.

The Hungarian is seated on the wall, between two pinnacles, legs dangling over a rope ladder fixed near him. At Rise he is counting the last strokes of the clock as it strikes.

HUNGARIAN

Ten—Eleven! Midnight.

(Jacopo enters approaching the door of the convent as if to knock on it. The Hungarian whistles in a sly way.)

Psst!

JACOPO

(Advancing toward the sound)

Is that you, by chance?

HUNGARIAN

Yes, it's me.

JACOPO

Eh! What the hell are you doing perched like a night bird atop that wall, instead of being with, the Duke—?

HUNGARIAN

Duke Alexander isn't at the convent of Santa Croce. He's with the Marchessa of Cibo.

JACOPO

At the home of the Marchessa instead of being at the convent?

HUNGARIAN

(sarcastically)

Stay there while I tell you milord's business from the

height of a ten-foot wall—come up here and you will know what you want to know.

JACOPO

(Climbing up and resting on the ladder)

What's happening?

HUNGARIAN

The simplest thing in the world—the death of a nun has set the whole community in commotion. Fra Leonardo is there. The good Abbess thanking His Highness for the honor she wished to do him, begged him to stay another day—or rather another night.

JACOPO

And His Highness was agreeable to this?

HUNGARIAN

His Highness quite simply wanted to throw out the dead body and the monk who watched over it. But good Catholic that I am, I slid up to him, and whispered in his ear that it would be better to leave these poor nuns in peace, and go pay a surprise visit to the Marchessa Cibo. "Heavens, it's time," milord replied—"I was forgetting the dear Marchessa." And as he had only to cross the square—he crossed the square.

JACOPO

But the Duke can't be amused to climb up by your ladder.

HUNGARIAN

Truly, no! The husband is away, and His Highness entered boldly through the door. It's his cousin, Lorenzino, prudent man, as you know, preferring two sentries to one—posted me here in case of accident.

JACOPO

I recognize our favorite very well there.

HUNGARIAN

Hush!

JACOPO

There! Coming from that side!

(The Marquis Cibo and Selvaggio Aldobrandini pass in the distance enveloped in large cloaks.)

SELVAGGIO

Knock carefully so the neighbors don't hear us.

CIBO

No need! I have the key.

SELVAGGIO

Then everything is going well.

(They move off with Cibo)

HUNGARIAN

Hum! What does that mean?

JACOPO

That means there are two honest Bourgeois who are going home, and that one of them is a prudent man who has his house key in his pocket.

HUNGARIAN

Yes—but—which house is it? Get down and look a bit where they're going—I have a suspicion.

JACOPO

What?

HUNGARIAN

Get down quickly, I say, and look.

(Jacopo jumps to the ground, runs quickly to the corner of the street then returns frightened.)

JACOPO

Hey! Hungarian!

HUNGARIAN

Well?

JACOPO

You made no mistake.

HUNGARIAN

How's that?

JACOPO

They went into the first door on the left.

HUNGARIAN

Into the Cibo palace?

JACOPO

Into the Cibo palace, exactly.

HUNGARIAN

The devil!

JACOPO

The Duke is alone?

HUNGARIAN

Eh! No—he is with his damned cousin, I already told you that.

JACOPO

And I asked the question again, because being alone or with him—it's all the same.

HUNGARIAN

Not so. It's worse.

JACOPO

Then run warn him.

HUNGARIAN

And if I disturb him unnecessarily, I will be well received, won't I?

JACOPO

Is he armed?

HUNGARIAN

He has his coat of mail and his sword.

(listening)

JACOPO

Do you hear something?

HUNGARIAN

Alert! Alert!

JACOPO

What's wrong?

HUNGARIAN

There's fighting.

JACOPO

Yes, I hear the clash of swords.

HUNGARIAN

They are attacking milord. You Jacopo, by the gate of

Torta street. You will find a crowbar at the foot of the ladder—I shall be over here.

(Drawing his sword and dropping to the other side of the wall.)

Hold firm—milord, hold firm! I am here!

(Lorenzino appears, masked at the top of the wall. He slides down the ladder rapidly, silently crossing the stage. From under his cloak, he pulls off a coat of mail, and he hurls it into the well. Then returns to listen at the foot of the wall. A cry is heard then nothing.)

LORENZINO

One of the two is dead. But which?

(The Duke appears at the top of the wall holding his sword between his teeth. Seeing Lorenzino at the foot of the ladder, the Duke shrugs his shoulders, takes his sword; shakes it so as to drain off the drops of blood, then puts it back in its scabbard, and folds his arms across his chest.)

DUKE

(in a calm voice)

By God, you are a famous companion, Lorenzino. Two men attack us, and I not only have to do my work but yours, too!

LORENZINO

Ah, milord, I thought that was a thing we had agreed upon.

DUKE

(coming down the ladder)

What? What was agreed?

LORENZINO

That I was your companion in your parties, your pleasures, and your love affairs—But not your battles? Oh, no! What do you want? You must take me as I am or leave me to others!

DUKE

(jumping to the ground)

Poltroon!

LORENZINO

Yes, poltroon! poltroon! Whatever you like—But I have, at least, on my side the advantage of not hiding any poltroonery. Anyway, do I have a coat of mail like yours, to give me courage?

DUKE

(raising his two hands to his breast)

Heavens! You are making me think—I left mine in the Marchessa's room.

(starts back up the ladder)

LORENZINO

Where are you going?

DUKE

To get it back. By God.

LORENZINO

Your Highness must have the devil in you! What, for a wretched coat of mail you would expose yourself?

DUKE

It's worth the trouble. I've never found one that fit me like that. It is so supple against my body that I feel it no more than a doublet of silk or velour.

LORENZINO

Good! The Marchessa will bring it to you or you will send for it. Do you know the Marchessa would be very beautiful in mourning? Which of the two did you kill? I really hope it was the Marquis.

DUKE

My word, I think I killed them both.

LORENZINO

Ah, the second, too? Really, gallows bird that you are!

DUKE

Wait! Here's the Hungarian who is going to give us news.

(The Hungarian appears at the top of the wall)

DUKE

Well?

HUNGARIAN

Well, milord, one is dead, and the other isn't much better. Does you Highness want me to finish the job?

DUKE

Not at all. The silence these men observed in attacking us makes me suspicious. I am sure one is the Marquis Cibo, and I think I recognized the other one for

Selvaggio Aldobrandini who is exiled from Florence. If it was he, his return is no accident, it would be a conspiracy. You will inform the Chancellor, and order him to arrest the wounded man.

LORENZINO

Milord, now my opinion is we should go to the Via Largha. One man killed, another man wounded the same night, seems to me to be enough.

DUKE

Anyway, we have nothing good to do here.

(starts to leave by the right)

LORENZINO

Not that way, milord, I hear the steps of several persons.

HUNGARIAN

(coming down are detaching the cord ladder)

So do I.

DUKE

Ah! Ah! Hungarian, are you afraid in your turn ?

HUNGARIAN

Sometimes—And you, milord?

DUKE

Never—And you Lorenzino?

LORENZINO

Me? Always.

(They leave—by the left. Michel, Matteo and Filippo Strozzi enter from the right)

MICHEL

(to Strozzi)

Let's proceed cautiously. Excellency! It seems to me there were a lot of people in this square.

STROZZI

There's nothing surprising about that. Midnight was just striking as we entered by the Porto San Gallo, and the noise perhaps was made by those I gave the rendez-vous to.

MICHEL

It's possible.

STROZZI

Stroll around through the Via Torta and look as you pass if someone is in the Cibo Palace. I will wait for you, hidden in the shadow of this wall.

(Michel goes off)

You, Matteo, go to the house of my sister in the Via dei Alfani, announce my return to her—and find out if my daughter is still with her. If for some reason she thought it necessary to separate from her, let her tell me where her niece is.

MICHEL

Your Excellency's sister is a prudent lady—would she believe me and consent to reply without a word from you?

STROZZI

You are right.

(going to the Madonna, and by the lights placed before her, writing some lines on a page in one of his notebooks, which he gives to Matteo.)

So, now.

(Matteo goes off. Strozzi effaces himself along the wall. Lorenzino comes forward hesitantly, looks around him. Confidently, as he doesn't see anyone, he crosses the square and raps three times at the gate of a small house; then backs away and claps three times with his hands. At this signal, the window of the house opens and a young girl appears in it.)

YOUNG GIRL

(in a low voice)

Is that you, Lorenzino?

LORENZINO

Yes.

YOUNG GIRL

Wait.

(A second later the door opens and Lorenzino goes into the house.)

STROZZI

(who has watched this scene)

O Florence! Florence! under tyranny, as under freedom you are always the same city of mystery and love affairs. But will you again be the city of courage and devotion?

MICHEL

(running)

Excellency!

STROZZI

(brusquely awakened)

It's you! Do you bring some news?

MICHEL

Yes—but terrible.

STROZZI

Speak! You know you can tell me everything.

MICHEL

In returning home, with Selvaggio Aldobrandini the Marquis Cibo found Duke Alexander in his home. The Duke killed the Marquis and grievously wounded Selvaggio.

STROZZI

From whom do you have these details?

MICHEL

Not far from The Marquis' door I noticed a man pulling himself along with difficulty and leaning on the wall. I went to him. Then he let himself fall on a pillar saying, "If you are an enemy, finish me! If you are a friend, save me! I am Selvaggio Aldobrandini."

STROZZI

And, then?

MICHEL

I told him who I was and whom I serve, offering to help him. He begged me to lend him my arm and to take him to Messere Bernardo Corsini—which was quickly done. Messere Bernardo Corsini lives a short distance. Via del Palazzo. Arrived there, Selvaggio sent me back to you, to tell you to flee.

STROZZI

To flee! And why?

MICHEL

Because he cannot receive you in his house, as he agreed—obliged as he is to beg asylum for himself with another.

STROZZI

That's all right, Michel. In Florence there are thirty-nine Strozzi not counting me. That's thirty-nine doors open to me, and were I forced to withdraw to my own palace, it is strong enough to sustain a siege against all the troops of Duke Alexander.

MICHEL

The more humble the house, the more secure you will be, milord. Remember you are Filippo Strozzi and that your head is worth 10,000 Florins.

STROZZI

You are right, Michel.

MICHEL

And despite that. Your Excellency will stay?

STROZZI

Yes, but you don't have the same reasons to stay, that I do. You can leave. The guard who let us pass through the Porto San Gallo has not yet been relieved, so retreat is easy for you. Go then, Michel! I release you from you oath.

MICHEL

(shaking his head)

Milord, I thought that your Excellency knew me better. If you have reasons for remaining in Florence, I have mine for not leaving you. It's necessary that the thing I came for shall be accomplished.

(extending his hand towards the convent)

Besides, if I wanted to flee, a voice from the convent would stop me crying "Michel, you are a coward." Thanks, for your offer, milord, but if you had left, I would have asked you permission to remain.

(The Convent door opens)

Oh!

(Leonardo comes out)

STROZZI

Who is that monk?

MICHEL

A Dominican, Excellency.

STROZZI

And consequently a patriot. I must speak to him.

MICHEL

And I, too.

STROZZI

(going to Fra Leonardo)

Pardon me, father, but you belong to the convent of Saint Mark, don't you?

FRA LEONARDO

Yes, my son.

STROZZI

You knew Savonarola?

FRA LEONARDO

I am his disciple.

STROZZI

And his memory is dear to you?

FRA LEONARDO

I venerate him equally with holy martyrs.

STROZZI

Father, I am proscribed. The asylum which I counted on is shut to me. My head is worth 10,000 Florins. I am Filippo Strozzi. Father, in the name of Savonarola, I demand hospitality of you.

FRA LEONARDO

I have only my cell. It's that of a poor monk. Brother, it is yours.

STROZZI

Think that I bring proscription to you, possibly death.

FRA LEONARDO

They shall be welcome, coming from duty.

STROZZI

So then, father?

FRA LEONARDO

I told you, my cell is yours. I will precede before you, you will follow.

STROZZI

This very night I am going to knock at the gate of the convent of Saint Mark.

(The two men shake hands.)

MICHEL

(stopping Fra Leonardo in his turn)

Pardon, father.

FRA LEONARDO

What do you want, my son?

MICHEL

Amongst the nuns who inhabit the convent of Santa Croce, isn't there one called...?

(hesitating he passes his hand in front of his face)

FRA LEONARDO

Have you forgotten her name?

MICHEL

(with a bitter smile)

I would sooner forget my own—called Nella?

FRA LEONARDO

What are you to the poor child? Are you her relative, her friend? You weren't simply a stranger to her?

MICHEL

I was—I was her brother.

FRA LEONARDO

Then, my son, pray for your sister, who is in heaven.

MICHEL

(in a strangled voice)

Dead?

FRA LEONARDO

This morning.

MICHEL

Lord, Lord—you are great and merciful! After troubles on Earth, peace on high, after the sorrows of a day, eternal blessing—Could I see Nella, father?

FRA LEONARDO

They are taking her body tonight to the convent of

Santissima Annunziata where she asked to be buried. You can see her the moment she leaves here.

MICHEL

And—will she leave soon?

FRA LEONARDO

(pointing to the convent door which opens)

Here she is!

MICHEL

Thanks!

(Fra Leonardo moves away.)

(The penitents leave the convent bearing, a catafalque on their shoulders on which the body of Nella lies in the midst of flowers and crowned with roses. Michel who rushes to the cortege lets out a groan so deep that the penitents halt.)

MICHEL

Brother, a prayer!

ONE OF THE MONKS

Speak.

MICHEL

O my brothers, put down the body of this young girl for a moment! It contains the only heart which ever loved me in this world, and I wish, now that it has ceased to beat to honor it one last time for its love.

(The penitents place the body on the ground and make room for Michel to approach it. Michel goes to his knees and bows to the dead girl.)

It's true, isn't it, that your agony, poor child, was less sad than your existence? Isn't it true, that death, so feared by the happy is for the unfortunate only a pale, cold friend that cradles us in its arms like a good mother, and consoles us softly, in this eternal bed called the tomb? Instead of crying, I would do well, poor child, to thank the Lord who called you to him, shouldn't I? Goodbye Nella—Goodbye for the last time. I loved you, beautiful child of the earth. I adore you beautiful angel of heaven! Goodbye, Nella!

I had returned to Florence to avenge you, living or dead. Sleep peacefully—I won't make you wait.

(putting his lips to the face of the young child, stifling tears, then rising)

And now, thanks, brothers! You can give this beautiful lily to the earth from which it came. All is finished. I return the body and the soul into the hands of the lord.

(Crossing his arms on his breast, lowering his head, and finishing his prayer silently, in front of the Madonna. The funeral cortege moves on.)

(Matteo entered in the midst of the preceding scene, as Strozzi listened, leaning on the iron ornaments of the well.)

MATTEO

(going to Strozzi)

Master—

STROZZI

Ah, is it you, Matteo? Did you see who just passed by?

MATTEO

I was there.

STROZZI

Did you know this nun?

MATTEO

Yes, Excellency. She was the daughter of my colleague old Nicolas Lapo, a wool carder. I recall that a year or two ago, the rumor ran through Florence that Duke Alexander had taken her from the home of her father, and that some days after her disappearance, she had entered a convent. Since then, from what was said to me just now by one of the penitents, she's never stopped weeping and praying and this morning she died like a saint.

STROZZI

Yet another victim who is going to cry for vengeance against you at the throne of the Lord, Duke Alexander! God wills what the end shall be!

(after a silence)

Well, Matteo, did you see my sister?

MATTEO

Yes, Excellency.

STROZZI

What did she say to you? Look, speak quickly! Is my daughter in good health?

MATTEO

Your sister hopes so, at least.

STROZZI

What do you mean she hopes so?

MATTEO

As your Excellency thought, she hasn't been able to keep Signora Luisa in her home. When she sees you, she will tell you why.

STROZZI

But then—Luisa?

MATTEO

Is hidden in this very square, in a little house where she lives with old Assunta and where your sister has not dared to come to see her for two weeks past for fear of being followed.

STROZZI

And this little house?

MATTEO

It is situated between the Via della Fogna and that of Delurio.

STROZZI

(grasping his arm)

You are mistaken, Matteo! That isn't the address that my sister gave you.

MATTEO

I ask pardon, milord—

STROZZI

But she doesn't live alone in that house?

MATTEO

Alone—with old Assunta.

STROZZI

Without any other woman than that?

MATTEO

Without any other woman.

STROZZI

Oh, my God—!

MATTEO

In the name of heaven—what is wrong with you. Signor Filippo?

STROZZI

Nothing. Dizziness! Matteo, go wait for me on the plaza San Marco opposite from the convent of the

Dominicans.

(Matteo bows and exits)

(Michel is still praying in front of the Madonna. Strozzi covers his head with his hand and then advances towards his daughter's house. At the moment he's going to knock, the door opens and Lorenzino, appears. Strozzi grasps him by the collar.)

STROZZI

Who are you?

LORENZINO

(trying to get loose)

What do you want with me?

STROZZI

Didn't you hear me? I am asking you who you are?

LORENZINO

What's it to you?

STROZZI

It is so important to me that I intend to know this very instant.

(Tearing off his mask, at the same time, Strozzi hood falls)

LORENZINO

Filippo Strozzi!

STROZZI

Lorenzino!

LORENZINO

Wretch! What are you doing in Florence? Don't you know that there's a price on your head?

STROZZI

I've come to demand a reckoning from Duke Alexander for the freedom of Florence and from you for my daughter's honor.

LORENZINO

(laughing)

If you had only come back, for this object it would be easy to arrange, my dear uncle, for the honor of your daughter is as intact as if her jealous mother kept it with her in her tomb.

STROZZI

Lorenzino leaves my daughter's at two in the morning and Lorenzino says my daughter is still worthy of her father? Lorenzino lies.

LORENZINO

(half sad, half joking)

Poor old man whose exile and misfortune have made him lose his memory! But have you forgotten something, Strozzi? It's that you married Julia Sodarina; it's that Luisa and I were destined for each other, it's that your wife, while the saintly creature was alive, made no distinction between me, Pietro and Tomasso, your two sons. What's surprising that I continue to love Luisa and she continues to love me, since our love was approved by you yourself?

STROZZI

(passing his hand over his face)

It's true, I had forgotten all that—but, by making an effort, I recall everything—all, rest assured. Heavens, here is my memory returning to me. Listen! You are my nephew—yes, my wife and I considered giving Luisa to you, yes, we made no distinction between you and our other children. Well, Lorenzino the promised day has arrived: You are twenty-five; Luisa is sixteen!

Proscribed as I am, isolated as she is, she needs someone to love her at the same time like a husband and a father. Luisa is the only wealth that has not been taken from me by either tyranny or exile. She is the only angel that still prays for me on earth. Well, my only angel, my only hope, my only wealth—I give you all that, poor prospect that I am—Marry my daughter, make her happy, and what ever may be the price of the treasure I shall have given you, I think that we are quits, but I still regard myself as your debtor.

LORENZINO

(shaking his head sadly)

You know quite well, Strozzi that what you propose to me now, once possible, possible perhaps in the future, is impossible today.

STROZZI

Oh, I knew your response in advance, Lorenzino! Why isn't it possible? Speak! God will give me the patience to listen to you, and I am listening.

LORENZINO

Look, how can you expect me, the favorite, the friend, the confidant of Duke Alexander to marry precisely the daughter of a man who three years since conspired against him, who twice tried to assassinate him, and who, banned from Florence, knowing a price has been placed on his head, returns tonight to attempt once more, according to all appearances some folly of the same type? For I label folly, you understand Filippo, all attempted conspiracies that do not succeed. Succeed! And what I label folly I will call wisdom—Marry your daughter? Marry Luisa Strozzi? For that I would have to be crazier than you are.

STROZZI

O my god, my god, what have you reserved for me! And still I am going through to the very end—Lorenzino—just now you called on my memory, and as you had seen my memory was faithful. Let me, in my turn, invoke yours.

LORENZINO

Strozzi, Strozzi I warn you I have forgotten so many things and there are many others which I do not wish to recall.

STROZZI

Oh! There is still some, you will recall, I hope, for it concern to your very life—The advice you received from your father, and the hopes of the youth, you would give to your country.

LORENZINO

Go, Filippo, go!

STROZZI

Lorenzino, has such a change been able to take effect in you that the present has so quickly squandered the promises of the past? Can the enthusiast for Savonarola allow himself to become the complaisant flatterer of a bastard of the Medici?

LORENZINO

Continue, I am making note of your every word to reply to you.

STROZZI

Can you, who, at nineteen, wrote a tragedy about Brutus, five years later play the role of sycophant at the court of Nero? No, it's impossible, isn't it?

LORENZINO

You are mistaken, Filippo, all that is true. But since we are recalling the past—my turn to question. Who oppressed Florence? Pope Clement the Seventh? Who, dreaming not only of the liberty of Tuscany, but a great Kingdom of Italy twice suggested you—assassinate Clement the Seventh—Even though he was pope? What did my protector say? To me! In refusing, you said,

"Strike if you wish, but we will let you take the crime on your account." And when Florence was under siege, when she had been taken, in your supreme wisdom you recognized that a Medici alone could reign, who told you. "I am the son of Pietro Francesco dei Medici, second nephew of Lorenzino, brother of Cosimo, son of Maria Sodarini, that woman of Exemplary sagacity, that old Roman, that Cornelia! I will reestablish the Republic—I swear it on my honor?" I did! And on my honor I would have done it or died trying. But no—you preferred the son of a Moor—a bastard of the Elder branch—and when I said, "Are you certain of it? His mother herself knows no more than the others." You abandoned me—The pure of conscience—of immaculate blood—and as I had a frail and feminine body you called me a Lorenzino, a Lorenzaccio! You slandered my life without being able to speak ill of it. Finally, you broke with Duke Alexander. But by then, many things became necessary. It was necessary that the first Gonfalonier Carducci, with Bernardo Castiglione and four others be decapitated; that the Second Gonfalonier, Raphael Gicolamo be locked in the Pisa Cathedral and perish there—poisoned, that the Preacher Benedetto Torano be delivered to Clement the Seventh, thrown into the Castel Saint Angelo and die there of starvation! It was necessary that five hundred fifty citizens, the first and most worthy in the city be exiled. It was necessary that the new Duke surround himself with foreign troops and name Alexander Villie, a foreigner, their chief—and Guiccardini, a traitor governor of

Bologna, conjointly with The Pope! It was necessary that he poison Cardinal Hippolito de Medici, his elder. It was necessary that he marry the daughter of the Emperor, Marguerite of Austria. Despite this marriage, he continues in his senseless debauchery, dishonoring the most sacred convents and the noblest families in Florence! When I saw all this, when I perceived nothing was obtained except by baseness, flattery, and corruption, that all righteous spirit, all generosity was forgotten or scorned, I returned to Florence, I became a courtier, friend, slave and companion of the debauches of Duke Alexander, and not being able to arrive at the first place in glory, I became the second in shame. Wasn't that well calculated—tell me, Filippo?

STROZZI

(seizing his arm)

Lorenzino! Lorenzino! Could what some are saying in whispers be true?

LORENZINO

And what is being said?

STROZZI

That, like the first Brutus, you counterfeit stupidity, but that, every evening, like him, you kiss the earth of our Mother Commune, begging your country to pardon the appearance in favor of the reality? Well, listen, if that's the way it is, Lorenzino, the time to throw off the mask has come. There are still crowns for Harmodius, and palms for Aristogeiton. Only there is not a minute to lose, if you want to be part of this great work I am preparing. After tomorrow it will be too late. Lorenzino, you've got a lot to do to become Lorenzo once again. Well, I take all your past on myself. And I will make you a halo for the future. I will open our ranks, I will give you my place—there are 300 of us who have sworn to die or set Florence free. March at our head, lead us, and I will be the first to give the example of obedience to others.

LORENZINO

(breaking out laughing)

Do you know, Strozzi, you have a marvelous idea there. You come to offer to me, Lorenzino the King of feasts, the Prince of happy days, the hero of mad nights of folly—the leading role in a twisted, dark, Roman conspiracy, mysteriously hatched in the shadows like that of Cataline, with oaths exchanged over a dagger and blood drunk from a cup! No dear friend, no! When I become crazy enough to conspire it will be in a manner less sad, less lugubrious. And then how your magnificent republic of Florence rewards those who are devoured for her! Like a mother tender of her sons, like a mistress faithful to her lovers—Rival of Athens, she's been imitating her in every respect, even in ingratitude towards her most illustrious citizens. Look, let's count those that the Abyss has devoured. First, of all the Strozzi, who foreseeing the future wished to cut off the evil at its root. You were left to hang from the balcony of the Palazzo Vecchio. Savonarola, who wanted to create a republic such as Plato had dreamed of was allowed to burn in the square of the Signory! Again, Dante de Castiglione, was allowed to be poisoned in Itri. So, the rope, the stake, poison. That is the thanks Florence the Magnificent keeps for those who devote themselves to her! Thanks! No, no, Filippo, the best thing is not to conspire. Hear this: you must conspire alone, without friends, without confidants, and then, if you haven't had the disease of dreaming too much someday, you may be lucky enough to see your conspiracy succeed. You speak to me of taking your place, Strozzi, of putting myself at your head, of taking to myself, the sole supreme honor of the act? Do you want me to tell you how your enterprise will end? Before twenty-four hours have elapsed, you will all be in prison. You've hardly gotten to Florence, right? You've hardly set foot here. Well, one of you is already dead, another wounded. Orders have already been given for you to be arrested—from first to last. Oh, Strozzi follow good advice—a fool sometimes gives it! Go back the way you came, when you reach the Fortress of Montereggione, shut your gates, lower your portcullis, raise your drawbridge and wait!

STROZZI

And what do you want me to wait for?

LORENZINO

How should I know? Perhaps, one night, perhaps one night when you least suspect it, the breeze which blows so sweetly among the laurels of the Arno and the pines of the Cascines will bring you these liberating words; "Duke Alexander is dead!"

STROZZI

I wager ill, Lorenzino! of the three offers I have made you, you have refused two. But I hope you will indeed accept the third.

LORENZINO

If is less crazy than the first two, with delight—yes, Strozzi.

STROZZI

(drawing his sword)

That is to do me instant satisfaction for your offenses, your refusal, and your advice.

LORENZINO

Oh, this time you are decidedly mad, my poor friend! a duel with me—with me, Lorenzino! Do I fight? Is it not agreed, accepted, recognized that I do not have the strength to lift a sword, and that I become ill seeing a drop of blood run? But don't you know I am effeminate, a poltroon, a coward! Ah, my word, I thought I was better known since Florence cries my praise to all Italy, and Italy to the entire world. Thanks, Strozzi, you distrusted Florence in my favor, you alone could still do me this honor.

STROZZI

Yes, you are right, yes, Lorenzino—you are effeminate, a poltroon, a coward! Yes, Lorenzino, you are a wretch and you don't deserve to die by a hand like mine. Begone! I ask nothing more from you, begone! I expect nothing more from you. I only hope in God—begone.

LORENZINO

Well, finally! You've become reasonable again. Goodbye, Strozzi.

(he leaves)

STROZZI

Michel! Michel!

MICHEL

(approaching)

Here I am, master.

STROZZI

You see that man going off over there? You see him.

MICHEL

Yes.

STROZZI

Well, if tomorrow that man is not dead, we are lost! That man knows everything.

MICHEL

And what's his name?

STROZZI

Lorenzino de Medici.

MICHEL

Lorenzino! Lorenzino! The favorite of The Duke! Rest assured Signor Filippo, he will die.

STROZZI

That's fine—Go.

(Michel leaves. Strozzi walks, sword in hand sword, towards the house his daughter is living in, raises the knocker, but after reflecting lets it drop noiselessly.)

STROZZI

No, not tonight. Tomorrow! Tonight, I will kill her.

(He moves off)

(CURTAIN)

ACT II

Lorenzino's quarters. Two side doors, with a door at the rear. Busts, statues, medical instruments, manuscripts lying here and there.

Duke Alexander is taking a fencing lesson from a Master of Arms. Lorenzino, by a table is amusing himself by piercing gold sequins on the point of his sword.

DUKE

(to the Master)

Enough for today, I am tired: Till tomorrow! Go!

(The Master of Arms leaves. The Duke goes to Lorenzino.)

What the devil are you doing there?

LORENZINO

You see, milord: I am doing like you—weapons.

DUKE

What do you mean weapons?

LORENZINO

Doubtless: These are my weapons. This little knife is my sword, my saber, my rapier. You don't think that the day I have some complaint about someone, I will stupidly go find a way to quarrel with him and put him at the point of my sword while putting myself at the tip of his? Not so naive, my Prince! When one has the misfortune to be the favorite of a man as abominable as Duke Alexander, one must get from the situation all the benefits one can.—No, when that day comes, I will wait for my man and I will stick, my little knife in his throat.

(The Duke takes the knife and looks at the handle.)

Oh—it's not the handle to admire, it's the blade. See, sharp as a needle and strong like the two handed sword of your enemy, Francis the First.

DUKE

And where did you buy this masterpiece?

LORENZINO

Buy! Can one buy such marvels. My cousin Cosimo of the Black Band gave it to me. Imagine, the poor child bored in his castle at Trebbio, so he practices Chemistry. He invented a way of poisoning cats and tempering steel. With his poison the strongest cats are dead within five seconds, with his steel, he can cut marble. The last time that I visited him, can you guess who I found with him? Benvenuto Cellini who refused to work for you. He was then, boasting, horrible Gascon that he is, of having fired the arquebus that killed the Constable de Bourbon. He brought this knife to Cosimo, who gave it to me. So, blade by Cosimo, mounted by Benvenuto Cellini it ought to kill by itself. I would offer it to you, but what has been given must be kept, and then I need my little knife. I have someone to kill.

DUKE

You are good to give yourself that trouble. Tell me who annoys you and I will rid you of him.

LORENZINO

Ah, Milord, how indelicate you are in matters of vengeance! You would rid me of them by the hand of some hatchet man, right? Do you count as nothing the pleasure of avenging yourself, of feeling a little well tempered blade slide through an enemy and piercing his heart with this fine steel blade? Last night, didn't you have more pleasure in killing the Marquis of Cibo yourself when you punctured his two lungs than you would have by letting Jacopo murder him, who would brutally have cut his throat, or the Hungarian who would have stupidly split open his belly.

DUKE

Ah, by God! You are making me think. You know the second fellow wasn't dead?

LORENZINO

Bah!

DUKE

No. they followed the track of his blood from the Palazzo Cibo to the house of Bernardino Corsini, and they took his host with him. It was no more difficult than that.

LORENZINO

And who was the other one?

DUKE

Selvaggio Aldobrandini. A very clever man, timely, is this Morizio, my Chancellor of the week, admit it my precious.

LORENZINO

Yes, yes, yes—But doubtless this clever man told you something more.

DUKE

I didn't ask him anything else.

LORENZINO

Good: a Chancellor should only answer questions that are asked. The Signor Morizio thinks the Marquis of Cibo and Selvaggio Aldobrandini returned to Florence alone?

DUKE

He thinks so, yes.

LORENZINO

He didn't, by chance, mention Filippo Strozzi?

DUKE

Indeed, I even asked him where Strozzi was—positively.

LORENZINO

Ah! And where is my dear uncle?

DUKE

In his fortress of Montereggione.

LORENZINO

Well, I see I was deceived on the account of my friend Morizio.

DUKE

In what?

LORENZINO

Why in thinking he was stupid but decidedly, I see he's merely an imbecile.

DUKE

What changed your opinion?

LORENZINO

The way he's informed.

DUKE

What do you mean! Filippo Strozzi?

LORENZINO

Left Montereggione yesterday, at three in the afternoon.

DUKE

To go where?

LORENZINO

To come to Florence.

DUKE

To Florence?

LORENZINO

Why put himself out?

DUKE

Strozzi in Florence?

LORENZINO

The fact is, he's a person of too little consequence for his comings and goings to concern anyone. He's only the head of the dissidents, that's all! Hasn't he twice tried to assassinate Your Highness? Once by filling with gun powder the chest you are accustomed to sit on for he was forewarned that Your Majesty wore this coat of mail. Ah, by the way—have you been able to find your coat of mail. Milord?

DUKE

Impossible to put hands on it!

LORENZINO

You must entrust Morizio with making a search for it. With him, nothing can be lost.—Except the outlaws but by luck I found them.

DUKE

What the devil do you say?

LORENZINO

I say, milord, if you didn't have your poor Lorenzino to watch over you many beautiful events would occur.

DUKE

And I am the more grateful to him for watching over me, since, if the throne were vacant he would mount it.

LORENZINO

Milord, I only value a throne that I can not only sit on but also sleep on.

DUKE

Really Lorenzino, I must tell you one thing. I think

you are my only friend.

LORENZINO

I am enchanted to find myself of the same opinion as you, milord.

DUKE

And if I was a man to pride myself on someone that someone would be you. But for that, you would have to serve me as well in love as in politics.

LORENZINO

And if I served Your Highness as well in love as in politics?

DUKE

Then you would be a precious man, incomparable, inestimable; a man that I would not swap, were I given Naples in return, against the First minister of my father in law Charles the Fifth who pretends to have the best ministers in the world.

LORENZINO

God! That's how poorly I serve milord in love.

DUKE

Ah, yes—be boastful! It's already a month that I ordered you to find the retreat of this little Luisa, who has escaped me, I don't know how, and of whom I am madly amorous—I don't know why—and I am no further advanced than the first day. But I warn you, I have loosed my best trackers on her spoor.

LORENZINO

Truly, milord I must agree I am a big ninny.

DUKE

You?

LORENZINO

Yes, me! What! I didn't give you news of her?

DUKE

You have not said a single word, traitor!

LORENZINO

Not a traitor—but forgetful—I've been back on her track for three days.

DUKE

Really, Lorenzino, on my oath, I don't know what keeps me from strangling you.

LORENZINO

Plague! At least wait till I have given you the address.

DUKE

Where does she live, torturer?

LORENZINO

Near the convent of Santa Croce, between the street of De Lucca and that of the Fogna—about twenty paces from the Marchessa. Eh, by god last night if you had known, after having come down from the wall, you would have returned with your ladder and climbed up the balcony of the other one.

DUKE

That's fine. Tonight, I am going to carry her off.

LORENZINO

Ah, milord, I recognize you there, with your Moorish customs.

DUKE

Lorenzino!

LORENZINO

Pardon, milord, but it's really true you lack gravity and prudence. What the devil! These are distinctions to be made between women—they are not all to be attacked in the same manner. There are some to be carried off and who find that quite natural—The Marchessa of Cibo is such a one—but there are others who have the pretension to be treated more gently and you must take the trouble to seduce them.

DUKE

Good! What's to be done?

LORENZINO

For example those who throw themselves out the window, seeing you enter through the door—like the poor daughter of that weaver whose name I cannot recall. It's with such manners that you drive your Florentines to inflamed protests, milord.

DUKE

Let the Florentines protest! I detest them.

LORENZINO

There you go again, falling back on prejudices against your own good people.

DUKE

Miserable silk merchants, evil carders of wool who make coats of arms from the signs of their shops. Who meddle in matters concerning my birth and try to cheat me of my birthright.

LORENZINO

(shrugging his shoulders)

As if one was the master of choosing his father.

DUKE

I find you are joking to take their side.

LORENZINO

Ah, yes, really I am paid for that.

DUKE

Wretches who insult me everyday!

LORENZINO

Of course, they spare me!

DUKE

Then why do you plead for them?

LORENZINO

So they don't complain against us. They are petitioners, your Florentines, they make them to everybody—to Francis the First, to the Pope, to the Emperor—They would, make them to the Devil, as you have the honor to be his son-in-law.

DUKE

How's that?

LORENZINO

To the Emperor! They would inform him of your amours, if they could so he would catch you and speak up for his daughter. Madonna Marguerite of Austria who is beginning to complain of being forlorn after ten months of marriage.

DUKE

Hum! Do you know, my boy, on that subject, you are not lacking in reason.

LORENZINO

By God! I am the only one in your court who is reasonable, milord. It's for that they all say I am mad.

DUKE

Ha!—So, in my place you would seduce Luisa.

LORENZINO

My word, yes! If only to change my approach.

DUKE

But you know what you are proposing is very boring and time consuming?

LORENZINO

Bah! A matter of five or six days.

DUKE

And how would you proceed, great seducer? Let's hear!

LORENZINO

I would begin by waiting till I knew where Strozzi is hidden.

DUKE

What! Wretch—you don't know?

LORENZINO

Ah, milord, you are very exacting! I give you the address of the girl, grant me twenty-four hours to discover that of the father. I can't do everything at once!

DUKE

Well, when I have the address of the father—

LORENZINO

You will arrest him and try him according to the law.

DUKE

Ah, as to that! You didn't warn me you were descended from the Consul Fabius.—You are for temporizing, today!

LORENZINO

Do you have something better to propose? Do it!

DUKE

Strozzi is proscribed. Strozzi returns to Florence. Strozzi puts himself in contravention of the law. Ten thousand Florins is the price on his head. Someone brings his head to my treasurer, my treasurer pays—that's all! I don't have to concern myself about it.

LORENZINO

Well, that's exactly what I feared.

DUKE

Why's that?

LORENZINO

Why because in that way, you ruin everything. That way can Luisa ever be anything to the murderer of her father? While by following the course that I propose to you, you arrest Strozzi, you have him condemned by the eight judges, this will give you an appearance of justice about which you care very little, I know indeed, but a tender daughter like Luisa will never let her father die when with a word, she could save him! All the odium of the condemnation falls on the judges. You, on the contrary, shine like ancient Jupiter, charged with bringing about a happy ending you arrive in a machine. The trick is sure.

DUKE

But devilishly hackneyed, my precious.

LORENZINO

Ha, by God! Are you putting some imagination into tyranny? Since Phalarus, who invented the brass bull, and Procrustes who invented beds that were too long and too short, there has truly been only one tyrant of genius—That was the divine Nero. Well, I ask you—how has posterity rewarded him? According to Tacitus, some pretended he was mad. According to Suetonius, others said he was a savage beast. Would you be a tyrant, after that? It would almost be better to be one of the mob—word of honor—There'd at least be some chance for the future.

DUKE

Five or six days, you say?

LORENZINO

Look, it's not my last word.

DUKE

So be it; but then I'll have to have Strozzi's address today.

LORENZINO

Get it from you Chancellor Morizio; that's his concern, not mine.

DUKE

Lorenzino, you promised me it.

LORENZINO

Did I promise it to you? In that case, you'll have it. Whatever I promise, I do.

(The Hungarian and Birbante enter.)

Why here are out two servants who seem to need to speak to us. They both come, probably, on behalf of the devil. Let's not make them wait, milord.

DUKE

Come, come Hungarian.

LORENZINO

Come, come in, Birbante.

(Each of the two servants speaks low to his masters.)

DUKE

(breaking out laughing)

You arrive too late to have the reward! Between the street of del Valeo and that of Fogna.

HUNGARIAN

And who told you the address, milord?

DUKE

A much clever bloodhound than you, my poor friend.

(pointing to Lorenzino)

HUNGARIAN

(Aside)

Ah, the demon! He only knows how to do injury to honest men.

DUKE

And you Lorenzino—what is it?

LORENZINO

A masked lady, your Highness, and who doesn't want, it seems, to remove her mask except to your servant.

(Birbante leaves)

DUKE

Lucky scoundrel! That smells of aunt Ginora—a mile off.

LORENZINO

Well, what could be more moral than an aunt who comes to visit her nephew?

DUKE

Especially, when the aunt is twenty-two and the nephew twenty-five. You know that I have a letch for her. Make her all sorts of promises on my part.

LORENZINO

I will promise her that you will dye your beard and hair.

DUKE

Why's that?

LORENZINO

Because she's told me that she only likes red heads—my sweet aunt.

DUKE

Wise-guy!

(going off with the Hungarian)

Let's see, come here—you still have something to say

to me.

HUNGARIAN

I admit it.

DUKE

Speak.

HUNGARIAN

To Your Highness alone.

DUKE

Speak low, then.

HUNGARIAN

Milord, the next time your devoted cousin comes down from a second floor by a rope let me cut the cord, I beg you.

DUKE

And why's that, if you please?

HUNGARIAN

Because I have an idea; it's that this man is betraying you.

DUKE

Cut the rope, Hungarian; you are master of that.

HUNGARIAN

(joyous)

Ha!

DUKE

Only, if you do that, I will order an executioner to take two ends of that rope and put your neck in a bow tie. Do you consider yourself warned?

HUNGARIAN

Yes, milord—Your Highness has said everything?

DUKE

Not yet—I promise a hundred gold Florins to the first who would give me Luisa's address.

HUNGARIAN

And I thought I had earned it.

DUKE

But I added that I would give fifty to the second.

(tossing him a purse)

Here, if there is more, you will give the difference to Jacopo.

HUNGARIAN

And if there is less?

DUKE

Then you will demand the balance from Lorenzino. He owes it to you for your good intentions towards him.

(He leaves by a side door and the Hungarian goes to the rear)

LORENZINO

(going to open a small door)

Enter, beautiful lady.

(Luisa enters, takes of her mask then throws herself in the arms of Lorenzino)

LORENZINO

Luisa! My God! Who has made you commit such an indiscretion to come to my place—in plain day?

(running to the opposite door and locking it while

speaking)

Do you know who just left here? Do you know who is still in the gallery? Do you know who may return at any moment? The Duke!

LUISA

Lorenzo! Lorenzo! He knows where I live!

LORENZINO

Who?

LUISA

The Duke.

LORENZINO

Fine! Is that all?

LUISA

Just heaven! Don't you realize that this may be the greatest misfortune that can happen to us?

LORENZINO

I have foreseen that circumstance, dear child, and my precautions have been taken in advance. Now, for I must know everything, tell me how it happened.

LUISA

This morning, while leaving Saint Annunziata, where I had been to hear mass, I was followed home.

LORENZINO

I strongly advised you not to go out unmasked.

LUISA

I had mine on, Lorenzo, but unaware that a man was there to spy on me, I took it off for a moment to make the sign of the cross with the holy water. The man was hidden behind the basin of holy water.

LORENZINO

In a way that you were recognized and consequently followed?

LUISA

To my home.

LORENZINO

You should have gone to the home of a friend, and gone out by a rear door.

LUISA

What do you want? I didn't think of it. When I saw I was being followed, I lost my head.

LORENZINO

And that man was the Hungarian.

LUISA

Assunta recognized him.

LORENZINO

I knew all this.

LUISA

How could you?

LORENZINO

I told you, the Duke was here just now and the Hungarian made his report in front of me.

LUISA

Well—?

LORENZINO

Well—you mustn't be worried, dear child of my heart.

LUISA

Not worried? Impossible!

LORENZINO

You have at least three days and three nights before you.

LUISA

Three days and three nights.

LORENZINO

Yes, and in three days and three nights, many things can happen.

LUISA

But remember in recommending the precautions which would hide my retreat from all eyes you told me a hundred times you would prefer to die than to see it discovered.

LORENZINO

Yes, for at the time there was an enormous danger.

LUISA

And now there isn't any?

LORENZINO

There is; but it is much less.

LUISA

Then you are not terrified that the Duke may know where I live?

LORENZINO

I gave him your address before the Hungarian gave it to him.

LUISA

Lorenzo, I am looking at you, I hear you, and I don't understand you.

LORENZINO

You believe in me, Luisa?

LUISA

Oh, yes.

LORENZINO

In that case, what need is there for you to understand me?

LUISA

I would like to read your heart!

LORENZINO

Ask anything of God, but that, poor child.

LUISA

Why's that?

LORENZINO

Because you would be leaping over an abyss—and abysses cause vertigo.

LUISA

Lorenzino!

LORENZINO

You, too!

LUISA

No—my Lorenzo, my beloved Lorenzo.

LORENZINO

And now, was this all the news you had to bring me, Luisa?

LUISA

Do you already know the rest?

LORENZINO

That your father is in Florence, right?

LUISA

My God!

LORENZINO

You see, I know it.

LUISA

How do you know everything?

LORENZINO

I know that you are an angel and that I love you.

LUISA

This morning a monk came to tell me this joyous and terrible news—and he spoke to me at length of you and of our love.

LORENZINO

And you admitted nothing to him?

LUISA

Indeed—but under the secret of confession,

LORENZINO

Luisa! Luisa!

LUISA

There is nothing to fear: that monk was Brother Leonardo—the student of Savonarola.

LORENZINO

Luisa! I am afraid for myself—anyway, you haven't seen your father?

LUISA

No—the monk told me that my father didn't want to see me yet.

LORENZINO

Well, I am much luckier than you, for I've seen him.

LUISA

You?

LORENZINO

Yes.

LUISA

When was this?

LORENZINO

Yesterday evening.

LUISA

Where?

LORENZINO

By the door to your house, where he had seen me enter, and by which he was waiting for me when I left.

LUISA

And you spoke to him?

LORENZINO

Yes.

LUISA

Great God—what did he say to you?

LORENZINO

He proposed that I marry you.

LUISA

And?

LORENZINO

And I refused him.

LUISA

Refused, Lorenzo?

LORENZINO

Refused.

LUISA

You still love me?

LORENZINO

It's because I love you that I refused.

LUISA

My God—will you always be an eternal mystery for me. Will you never explain to me—?

LORENZINO

The hour hasn't come. You know all that they say about me in Florence?

LUISA

Yes—but I've never believed a word of it I swear to you.

LORENZINO

Don't pretend to be stronger than you are. More than once, you have doubted.

LUISA

When you weren't there, it's true; but as soon as I saw you, as soon as I heard the sound of your voice, as soon as I saw your eyes fixed on mine, as they are right now, I said to myself, "The world deceives itself, but my Lorenzo does not deceive me."

LORENZINO

And you are right, Luisa! And judge what I suffered when, seeing the treasure of all my hopes offered to me, having only to make a sign with my head, and it was mine, having only to extend my hand to seize it, I refused. Yes refused what at another time I should have paid my life for. What I suffered last night, Luisa! What bitter tears I devoured, what unheard of sufferings I dissimulated—you don't know—you will never know! Poor child! May God keep from your blessed face the shadow of calamities, of miseries, of shame which he has loaded on mine.

LUISA

But, still, still—why did you refuse?

LORENZINO

Because I have the strength to sustain the humiliation which weighs on me. But what I can suffer for myself, I will not suffer for the person I love. The person I love must have a chaste face, pure, smiling—that virginal chastity, that angelic purity—that unalterable serenity—that I've found in you.

(sighing)

Well, by becoming the wife of Lorenzo you will lose all that.

LUISA

But a day will come, won't it, Lorenzo when between us there will be no impediment nor mystery? A day will come when, in the face of all, we can confess our love?

LORENZINO

(placing one hand on his heart and raising the other to heaven)

Oh, yes; and I hope that day is not far off.

LUISA

Ah, that will be a beautiful day for me, my friend.

LORENZINO

And a great day for Florence! No queen ever mounting her throne, will have a cortege of joy and acclamations such as yours! If God and your love do not fail me. The dreams of joy you have for that day, however brilliant they may be—will still be far from the reality.

LUISA

So then—if my father calls me?

LORENZINO

Go boldly to him—tell him of our chaste and pure love—tell him especially of my profound and eternal love.

LUISA

And the Duke?

LORENZINO

Don't worry about him; That's my concern.

(A soft knocking can be heard at the door in the distance.)

LUISA

They are knocking at that door.

LORENZINO

(covering her with her cape)

Don't budge!

BIRBANTE

(outside)

Milord.

LORENZINO

What's wrong?

BIRBANTE

It's an actor who, having heard you wish to put on a tragedy for the pleasure of his Highness Duke Alexander, asks to be engaged in your troupe.

LORENZINO

Fine, let him wait. When he sees the door open he can enter.

(to Luisa)

And, you, my child, put your mask on, so that no one will know you came here—go through this room—a secret stairway will lead you to the court.

LUISA

Goodbye, my Lorenzo! When will I see you again?

LORENZINO

Tonight, probably. By the way, Luisa, where is your father? You hesitate? I understand. It's not your secret; be silent!

LUISA

It's not a secret for you, Lorenzo! My father is in the Convent of Saint Mark—in the cell of Fra Leonardo! Goodbye!

(She puts on her mask and hurries out)

LORENZINO

(Lorenzino assures himself that Luisa has gone while

looking at the half opened door. Then he opens the door in the rear. Michel waits in the antechamber.)

Enter.

(Lorenzino comes to the front of the stage, Michel enters, Lorenzino watches him distrustfully)

It's you who asked for me?

MICHEL

(taking a step forward)

Yes, milord.

LORENZINO

(extending his hand toward him)

A moment, friend! I have a policy that people who don't know each other more than we do—ought always to speak at a distance.

MICHEL

I beg milord to believe I know too well how much distance separates me from him, to be the first to shorten it.

LORENZINO

What! Wise-guy—do you pretend to have wit, per chance?

MICHEL

My word, milord, so much wit passed through my mouth when I played your comedy Alidorio—That it's not surprising some scraps remain in my speech.

LORENZINO

Oh! Oh! Flattery! I warn you, old boy, that the role of flattery here is employed in double, and triple, so if you counted on taking the lead on that score, you can go back where you came from.

MICHEL

Plague, milord, rest assured—I know better what I owe to my colleagues the courtiers than to walk in their tracks: no—I play the leading roles and leave the role of valets to those who wish to take them.

LORENZINO

The leading roles in tragedy or comedy?

MICHEL

Tragic or comic—indifferently.

LORENZINO

And what roles have you played? Let's see!

MICHEL

I played at the court of good Pope Clement the Seventh who had such marvelous friendship for you, milord—the part of Callimaco in the Mandrogola of Messire Machiavelli. Benvenuto Cellini who assisted at this presentation, could give you testimony of the success I had. Then at Venice, I filled the role of Ninco Parabolano in the Courtier, and if the illustrious Michaelangelo ever regains enough courage to return to Florence, he will tell you I almost made him die of laughter. So much so that he was ill for three days with the pleasure he received that night. Again, at Ferrara, I played in the tragedy of Sophonisba, the part of the tyrant, with such a natural touch that the Prince Hercules D'Este kicked me out the same evening from his duchy under the pretext that I had sought a success through innuendo, which happened without any attempt on my part—word of honor.

LORENZINO

Ah, indeed—if I am to believe you, you have a talent of the first order?

MICHEL

You don't have to believe me, you can test me, milord. But if you want to see me truly at my best role, permit me to play you a scene from your tragedy Brutus—a superb work—but which unfortunately is forbidden in all the countries where they speak the language in which it is written.

LORENZINO

And what is the role you've chosen in this masterpiece?

MICHEL

By Bacchus!—How can you ask? That of Brutus!

LORENZINO

Yeah! You say that in a tone that smells of republicanism a mile off! Were you, by chance, for Brutus?

MICHEL

I? I am neither for Brutus nor for Caesar. I am an actor, that's all. Long live great roles! With your permission I will let your Excellency hear me in the role of Brutus.

LORENZINO

Well, let's see—what are you going to recite for me?

MICHEL

The big scene of the fifth act—would you like it?

LORENZINO

The one at the end of which Brutus knifes Caesar.

MICHEL

Exactly.

LORENZINO

Go for the big scene then!

MICHEL

But, if Your Excellency wants me to display all my ability, he must give me the replies himself.

LORENZINO

Willingly—although I've forgotten the tragedies I created for the one I am by the way of creating—Ah, it's for the latter that I need an actor.

MICHEL

Well, here I am. Listen to me first of all. You will see what I am capable of.

LORENZINO

I am listening.

MICHEL

Let's see! We are in the vestibule of the Senate. Here's the statue of Pompey to your right. You are Caesar—I am Brutus. You are coming from the forum, I am waiting for you here. Does the mise-en-scène agree with you?

LORENZINO

Perfectly.

MICHEL

Wait while I drape myself in my toga. We're ready, aren't we?

LORENZINO

Yes.

BRUTUS (MICHEL)

Hold, Caesar! A word!

CAESAR (LORENZINO)

Speak Brutus, I am listening.

BRUTUS

Caesar, I came to wait for you on your way.

CAESAR

It is an honor for me to have so noble a client.

BRUTUS

You are mistaken, Caesar; I come as a suppliant.

CAESAR

You—suppliant?

BRUTUS

You know that all destiny by a double principle in its dominant birth sees good and evil share it's course, and that bad days follow happy days—with a step as certain as that we see in the career of the night following the day, and shadow following the light. Because, man—always envious, wishes to avoid the fate appointed for him by the Gods—whatever may be his genius. This torch which he believes an infinite light expires suddenly in his feeble hand, leaving him blind on the wayside. So as he reaches this high summit the first step he takes, rolls him into the abyss. Caesar, in the name of the Gods, listen to me, Caesar, hear me! For this man with a torch, ready to expire—it's you.

CAESAR

Yes, Brutus, you speak the truth. Yes, it's common law—But destiny does not have the same fortune for all. Each according to his heart makes his fate different. Where one stays small the other becomes great. All comes from the secret command which says to the servant; "crawl" and to the eagle, "fly." This command says to me— "March forward, Caesar. Your genius submitted to the unforeseen hazard, your building waits a last brick. And Caesar has done nothing until he does what there remains for him to do!"

BRUTUS

And what may Caesar wish to do? The Gauls are conquered, the Britons vanquished. Carthage is muzzled and roars in her chains. Egypt bleeds in the teeth of the Roman wolf. And the Euphrates is no more, having no more power over its waters than one of a thousand watering holes where we water our horses. Nothing dares resist us, all obstacles are effaced. The rebel of yesterday today asks for mercy. Be it advantage, hope, love, terror: All bow to your laws and your conquering eagle. Dominating the clouds where thunder growls, it's eyes on the sun, it soars above the world! What more must you do? What more do you want, you who—during your life we call divine? Is nothing enough? And must you punish Rome who in creating you has created more than a man?

CAESAR

Rome, of whom you are too zealous an advocate, has never spoken thus—and you know that, Brutus. No—Brutus is speaking for the nobility, which my name dazzles and my glory wounds. Especially since the day, when his fatal projects brought my titanic rival, Pompey, face to face with me on the field of Pharsalis. I injured the nobility by overthrowing Pompey; No, you know quite well that I am the people. The Gods have decided it.

BRUTUS

Caesar, Caesar, be silent! Peace and blessing to the great victim. For your victory, one day may become a crime. Beware then of insulting with a mocking smile the vanquished whose fall may destroy his conqueror. A ghost who will grow under the care of history to make his blood a stain on your glory. Your cause is yet to be judged. Today; the Gods were for you, but Cato was for him!

CAESAR

It appears that Brutus in his eternal hate has replaced the slave with the solemn voice who accompanies the Hero in the Triumphal Car—and comes to whisper to Caesar in the midst of the transports Rome is exploding with—"Remember Caesar—Caesar is only a man!"

BRUTUS

No, Caesar is a god if Caesar returns intact to the Romans the treasure they have put into his hands—But deaf to this advice, if Caesar betrays Rome, Caesar is no longer a God,—Caesar is less than a man, Caesar is a tyrant! But as you see me fall at your knees, as you hear me utter a last supreme cry, "Pity for the Romans, and pity for yourself." Then you will change your plans—O sadness—you do not reply to me.

CAESAR

(Repulsing Brutus)

Place to your Emperor!

BRUTUS

In that case, die, tyrant!

(Michel joining acts to his words, draws a dagger from his breast and strikes Lorenzino but the blade is blunted on the coat of mail that Lorenzino wears under his dress.)

MICHEL

(jumping back)

Ah! The Demon!—He's wearing armor.

(Lorenzino in his turn, rushes on Michel, seizes him by the waist, and after a silent but sharp struggle, overthrows him and places at his throat the little dagger of his cousin, Cosimo—then he bursts out laughing.)

LORENZINO

Ha, ha, ha. It appears the roles are reversed and it is Caesar who is going to kill Brutus. There! And now, I ask you, wretch—as they say to those condemned to death before reading the judgment have you something to say in you defense?

MICHEL

Nothing!—except that Duke Alexander ought to thank Heaven—for you are going to save his life.

LORENZINO

(pulling back his knife)

Huh? What do you mean by that?

MICHEL

One of those phrases that escape the mouths of the dying—Pay no attention and strike. I wish to die—kill me!

LORENZINO

Explain yourself first. You said something about Duke Alexander which interests me. Speak!

MICHEL

I said that Heaven does not want Florence to be free since it makes of you a shield for the tyrant.

LORENZINO

Why—then you want to kill Duke Alexander?

MICHEL

I have taken an oath that he will die only by my hand.

LORENZINO

Ah, here's something that changes the face of things completely.

(Releasing him)

Get up, sit down—and let's talk about this a bit.

MICHEL

(rising to his knees)

Lorenzino what's the good of playing with me? I

wanted to kill you. Call your men—send me to the gallows and everything will be finished.

LORENZINO

On my soul, I find you a pleasant rogue—to speak as if you were the master here! And if I have the caprice to let you live—who could prevent me from doing it?

MICHEL

Let me live?

(extending his hands toward Lorenzino)

You could let me live?

LORENZINO

Perhaps Michel de Tovalaccino!

MICHEL

You know my name?

LORENZINO

And perhaps your story, too, my poor Scoronconcalo; for you have two names—a man's name and a clown's name.

MICHEL

Well then, you understand why I want to kill Duke Alexander?

LORENZINO

Yes—Wasn't it a question of some young girl you wanted to marry? I don't know who she was.

MICHEL

Have you ever loved, Lorenzino?

LORENZINO

Me? Never! But one doesn't have to be mad to comprehend madness.

(Sitting in an armchair)

Look—tell me about it.

MICHEL

Well, I was in love—I was foolish enough for that. Duke Alexander's fool—I thought I retained the right to have a heart. Oh! You don't know what it is to cease to be a man to become a thing that laughs, weeps, grimaces, a thing on which everyone strikes to obtain a sound he likes—a puppet whose strings are pulled by the whole world. That's what I was, Lorenzino. Well in this somber degradation, in the midst of this dark night, one day, I saw a ray of sun shine: A young girl loved me! She was a sweet and beautiful child, pure and gay. The most chaste lily was less white than her face: a petal torn from the heart of a rose was less fresh than her cheek. She loved me! Me! Do you understand, sir? Me—poor buffoon, poor lonely empty headed!— Then, I had all the hopes of other men—I dreamed of intoxicating love—I divined the joys of family life. I went to find the Duke to ask his permission to get married. He broke out in laughter, "You marry," he cried, "you marry? But you are only a clown and look you've gone mad. Don't you know what marriage is? Haven't you noticed that since I married the daughter of the August Emperor Charles the Fifth, I am more difficult to amuse? Hardly would you be married, my dear Scoronconcalo, than you would become, sad, morose, troubled—once married you would cease to make me laugh. Come, come buffoon, enough on this subject—and the next time you speak to me of it I will give you twenty blows with the stick." The next day I mentioned it to him again. He kept his word—I was whipped bloody by Jacopo and the Hungarian. The next day I spoke to him of it again. "Come, I see the malady is inveterate," he said to me, "We must use extreme measures to cure you." Then, in the tone of a master who was interested in the sufferings of his servant he asked me the name of her I loved, her address, her family. I thought he had consented to my happiness. I threw myself at his feet, I kissed his knees, then I ran to Nella's home, and I spent a day with her of ineffable joy. That evening there was an orgy at the palace. The Duke was surrounded by his habitual companions. Francesco Guicciardini, Alexander Vitelli, and Andre Salviate—I was there, too—as I was at all feasts. When they were heated by the conversation, by the music, by the wine a door opened and they pushed into their midst a young girl. This young girl, this virgin, this martyr—she was the one I loved, for whom I would have given my life, my soul! It was Nella!

(throwing himself on his knees)

Oh let me live, milord—let me avenge myself—and on honor when I have strangled this tiger, I will return to lie at your feet, and I will give you my throat and say, "In your turn, Lorenzino, in your turn. Avenge yourself on me, as I have taken vengeance on him."

LORENZINO

(impassively)

But this isn't all?

MICHEL

What more do you want me to say? And what does the rest matter? I escaped from this cursed court, I ran until I had crossed the frontiers of Tuscany. In Bologna I found Filippo Strozzi. I knew him to be a mortal enemy of the Duke. I put myself in his service on the sole condition that when we returned to Florence, I would be the one who struck down the infamous Duke! Yesterday evening we returned. At the moment we passed before the Convent of Santa Croce, they brought forth the body of Nella dead of shame, of misery, of despair. Oh this time it's really too much.

LORENZINO

Yes, as to the rest, as to the order given by Filippo Strozzi to assassinate me because I wouldn't agree to marry his daughter—I understand. It's not worth the trouble to speak of it.

(after a moment of silence)

Well, answer me! If instead of calling my people and having you hanged, as you advised me yourself, just now, I give you your life, I give you your liberty?

MICHEL

Oh !

LORENZINO

But on a condition—you quite understand one doesn't do such mercy gratis.

MICHEL

This condition I accept—whatever it may be—I sign with my blood—I guarantee it with my life.

LORENZINO

(in a somber voice)

Michel, I too, I have to avenge myself on someone.

MICHEL

Oh! For you great lords that's very easy.

LORENZINO

Well that's what deceives you—for the one on whom I have to avenge myself is a familiar of the Duke—one of those who were at the orgy with Nella.

MICHEL

Oh! Yours, Lorenzino, I am yours. And if you are afraid I will escape or save myself, shut me in a cell—to which you alone have the key—with a chain on my foot, a collar on my neck—don't let me leave but to strike your enemy—but your enemy dead, leave me the Duke!

LORENZINO

So be it! But who will answer to me for your loyalty?

MICHEL

(extending his hand)

By the salvation of Nella! Now—what are your orders? What do you wish me to do?

LORENZINO

My word, whatever you like—Return to Strozzi who must be awaiting you with impatience—tell him it was impossible for you to get near me—that you didn't kill me today—but that you will kill me tomorrow.

MICHEL

And then?

LORENZINO

And then? Since you walk about every night—from eleven to one in the via Largha—that's all I ask of you.

MICHEL

You have nothing more to tell me?

LORENZINO

No—By the way—perhaps you need some money?

MICHEL

Thanks—But you could make me a gift, milord.

LORENZINO

Of what?

MICHEL

Let me take a sword from this trophy case.

LORENZINO

Choose it.

MICHEL

I will take this one, milord.

LORENZINO

Come, the rogue is a connoisseur.

MICHEL

So then—?

LORENZINO

In the Largha—from eleven at night to one in morning.

MICHEL

Tonight.

LORENZINO

Tonight and every night.

MICHEL

It's agreed, milord—count on me!

(He leaves)

LORENZINO

(alone)

By God I count very much. Truly, I think I am happier than Diogenes, and I have found the man I was looking for. Good—I was forgetting the main thing,

(he sits at a table and writes)

Filippo Strozzi is hidden in the cell of Fra Leonardo in the Convent of St. Mark.

(calling)

Birbante!

(Birbante appears.)

LORENZINO

To Duke Alexander!

(CURTAIN)

ACT III

The cell of Fra Leonardo. A door at the rear and a side door to the right of the spectator. To the left in the forestage a prie-dieu, further back a window. Above the door in the back a coronation of the virgin by Beato Angelo.

FRA LEONARDO

I tell you, Strozzi, you can still bless, love, embrace your child and pardon Lorenzino.

STROZZI

(agitated and crossing back and forth on the stage)

Lorenzino! But I told you he's loved by her—I told you I saw him leave her house at one in the morning; I tell you he's a wretch!

FRA LEONARDO

Luisa loves him, it's true, but with a pure and fraternal love.

STROZZI

The love of a Lorenzino, pure and fraternal? And it's you who tell me this, father? You, accustomed to read to the depths in the hearts of men—it's you who come to defend this infamous person against me!

FRA LEONARDO

(dreamily)

Yes, my son, as you said,—there are few souls I have not sounded—few of those somber pits which agitate human passions of which I have not measured the depths. Well, I will tell you, Strozzi—Lorenzino is one of those whose thoughts have always remained unknown. Now, I have for a long time watched the eyes of this man on whom reposes, as you know, the hopes of the country. Well, the more I've learned of this man, the less clearly I've been able to see the depths of his soul. Since his return from Rome he's become impenetrable to all scrutiny,—even to ours, for since his return, not a single time has he approached the tribunal for penitents.—Oh—the one who hears the supreme confession of this man!—

STROZZI

(in a thick voice)

Yes, if he isn't soon murdered without confession—

FRA LEONARDO

It doesn't matter—all is not lost with him, since he loves. Love is not only a belief but even a religion—and the heart in which a ray of love remains is not entirely denying of God.

STROZZI

(without listening to Fra Leonardo)

Am I unhappy enough! To complete breaking my heart, already so full of distrust, the love of this man rested on Luisa and that Luisa returns it.

FRA LEONARDO

Strozzi, Strozzi—instead of accusing heaven, on the contrary, thank it, for this poor child abandoned as she was and thinking to satisfy your paternal desire, while loving like a woman, remains pure like an angel!

STROZZI

Oh! If I believed that a least!

FRA LEONARDO

You may since I affirm it!

STROZZI

Then why doesn't she come to tell me this herself? It seems to me if it was she who told me, I wouldn't suspect her anymore.

LUISA

(entering through the door at the right and rushing to her father's arms)

Don't suspect me anymore, for here I am, beloved father.

STROZZI

(to Fra Leonardo who moves away)

You are leaving us, father.

FRA LEONARDO

Joy passes so quickly, Strozzi, that it's good while one man is happy that he have near him another who prays.

(he leaves)

STROZZI

(letting himself collapse in an arm chair)

Luisa, you are very late—But still you are here.

LUISA

Father, how much you must have suffered if it is true you suspected me.

STROZZI

Oh, yes, I have indeed suffered! For you will never know how much I love you, Luisa! The love of parents is a mystery between them and the Lord. For the three years since I left Florence, I've been able to get news of you only after long intervals. You and Florence, you are my only loves, and God forgive me, between Florence, my mother and you, my daughter, I believe it is still you that I love the best!

LUISA

My brothers were with you, father, and I was happy in the idea that they would console you.

STROZZI

Your brothers are strong men, strong to struggle, strong to suffer. When a father begets a son, he knows in the future he owes that son to his country. But a daughter belongs more intimately to her father; a daughter— she's the angel of a Christian house, she's the statue of virginal love that has replaced the penates of the ancients. Judge all I have suffered, my child, thinking of the dangers which threatened you in this unhappy

city, and when I consider my inability to protect you—
But you, you, my daughter—what have you been doing
during all this time?

LUISA

I've spent all this time, father divided between prayer
and love. I prayed for you father, I loved Lorenzo.

STROZZI

So—it's true—you love him?

LUISA

Past comprehension. If I were to lose him God himself
could not replace him in my heart.

STROZZI

But no one knows of your love?

LUISA

No one, father.

STROZZI

Where did he see you? How did he see you?

LUISA

Up to the moment he told me to leave my aunt, he saw me at my aunt's, and then after that for a while in that little house in the plaza Old Saint Maria. There he often came in disguise, but always masked. Each time we agreed to a new signal for the next time. He must have some great secret in his life that I don't know about; one day he will be triumphant and joyous, another somber and beaten. Sometimes he is gay like a child, sometimes he weeps like a woman!

STROZZI

And you?

LUISA

I—I am always gay or sad according to whether he is gay or sad.

STROZZI

And the marriage once arranged between you—does he still speak to you of it?

LUISA

Oh, yes, quite often, father—First he's exalted, then he speaks of the future: of power, of liberty, and I no more understand him than when he keeps silent—for his words are as mysterious as his silences.

STROZZI

(pulling her into his arms and shaking his head)

Oh, my child! My child!

LUISA

Reassure yourself, father—it's not Lorenzo that you have to fear.

STROZZI

Ah, yes you remind that another danger threatens you—this Duke—he loves you then?

LUISA

No one has told me that yet, but several times, and this very morning, I was followed by masked men—and I felt from the trembling of my heart that I was in peril.

STROZZI

He doesn't know where you live?

LUISA

He's known it for the last several hours.

STROZZI

Oh—my God.

LUISA

I was quite frightened at first, but later Lorenzo told me there was nothing to fear and I was reassured.

STROZZI

Lorenzo! Then you've seen him today?

LUISA

This morning, yes, father.

STROZZI

And he told you that yesterday evening we saw each other?

LUISA

He told me.

STROZZI

Did he tell you that I had offered him the honor of giving you to him as his wife?

LUISA

He told me.

STROZZI

Did he tell you that he refused?

LUISA

He told me all this.

STROZZI

What do you make of it, then?

LUISA

I felt compassion for him.

STROZZI

You felt compassion for him?

LUISA

I was thinking of what he must be suffering.

STROZZI

Where did you see him this morning?

LUISA

At his palace.

STROZZI

You were at his home—via Largha—in his infamous house?

LUISA

I thought the danger pressing.

STROZZI

Were you the first to speak of me?

LUISA

No—he was the first to speak of you to me.

STROZZI

He doesn't know where I am, does he?

LUISA

Excuse me, father, he knows it.

STROZZI

Who told him?

LUISA

Me.

STROZZI

Wretch! You've ruined me, and you've ruined yourself with me.

LUISA

Oh, father, how can you think?

STROZZI

And you, how can you be blind and credulous to this degree? By now, Luisa, Duke Alexander knows everything, and by this time, I, you, my friends, are in his power and it's your mad love it's your senseless love which has thrown us into his hand. Ah, wretch! May God pardon you as I pardon you—but what you've done!

LUISA

(supplicatingly)

Father! Father!

(A noise can be heard outside.)

STROZZI

Listen, listen!

(pointing to the direction from which the noise comes)

Do you hear?

(pulling his daughter to the window)

Here! Look, and still doubt.

LUISA

Bailiffs, soldiers! The Duke! Father, kill me—But no, it's impossible—you were betrayed,

STROZZI

Yes, I've been betrayed, and what is more terrible, I've been betrayed by my daughter.

LUISA

Oh! Wait, wait, father—before condemning us so—

FRA LEONARDO

(appearing at the door in the rear)

Brother, are you ready to be a martyr?

STROZZI

Yes.

FRA LEONARDO

That's fine—for the executioners are here.

DUKE

(outside)

Stay by this door—and don't let anyone in!

(in the doorway)

Ha, ha! I was indeed well informed—and here's the wolf taken in the trap.

FRA LEONARDO

(Rushing in front of the Duke)

Who are you? What do you want?

DUKE

Who am I? I am as you see, my worthy father, a pious pilgrim who visits houses of the Lord, to reward and punish those who in their pride believe themselves above rewards and punishments.

(pointing to Strozzi)

I have to speak to this man.

FRA LEONARDO

This man is the guest of the Lord, this man is sacred—You cannot get to him except by passing through my body.

DUKE

That's all right—we'll pass through you—Do you imagine that one who, to mount a throne, has marched over the body of a city will be stopped for fear of soiling his feet on the body of a miserable monk?

HUNGARIAN

(hand on his dagger)

Milord—is it necessary?

DUKE

No—it's not necessary—or at least, not yet. You are always in such a hurry.

(to Monk)

Come! Place to your Duke!

FRA LEONARDO

My Duke? I don't know that name. I know who Gonfalonier is—I know what the Republic of Florence is, but I don't know what a Duke is, I don't know what a duchy is.

DUKE

(between his teeth)

Enough! Place to your master.

FRA LEONARDO

My master—that's God! I have no other Lord than the one in heaven and while a voice from below says "Get out, I hear one from above which says "Stay."

HUNGARIAN

(gesturing)

Well?

DUKE

(to the Hungarian)

Wait! And when, by chance, I am patient, be so too! You see quite well I don't wish to frighten this young girl.

(to Fra Leonardo)

Well—monk—since you know neither Duke nor master—place to the stronger!

(The Hungarian and Jacopo take the monk by the arms and pull hum away. The Duke finds himself face to face with Strozzi who pushes his daughter away with his hand.)

STROZZI

Duke Alexander, I thought you had enough with your chancellor, your jailers, and your guards not to play yourself the role of bailiff. I see I was wrong.

DUKE

Do you count for nothing the pleasure of meeting your enemy face to face? Do you take me for one of those who slip by night into the city, who hide by day in a dark hole, who wait patiently and treacherously for the hour to stretch his arm in the shadows and to strike from behind? No. I march in the clarity of the sun and I come to tell you at high noon, "Strozzi, we've played against each other a terrible role—life was the stake—you've lost, Strozzi—pay up!"

STROZZI

Yes, and I admire prudence of the gambler who comes to claim his debt so well accompanied.

DUKE

Oh, really? Do you think I am afraid? Do you think I would not have taken you alone, anywhere I could hope to meet you? Ah, you make a strange error, and you take me for someone else.

(to Jacopo and the Hungarian)

Leave—shut the door after you—and don't come unless I call you—whatever you hear even if it is my death cry.

(The Hungarian wants to make a remark)

Ah! Obey!

(Jacopo and the Hungarian obey.)

DUKE

Well—here I am alone, Strozzi! alone against the two of you—Ah, yes, I understand: I am armed and you are without arms—Wait. Here, Strozzi I throw this sword.

(he unbuckles his sword and throws it behind him)

Here Strozzi I offer, you a dagger—Take it, Old Roman—Wasn't there in antiquity, a Virginius who killed his daughter—a Brutus who killed his King? Make yourself immortal like them. Come—choose and strike. But strike—What do you risk? Not even your head. You know very well it belongs to the executioner and you, monk, what stops you? Take up this sword and come strike me from behind if your hand trembles to strike me facing me.

FRA LEONARDO

My God forbids his ministers from spilling blood. But for that, you would have been dead a long time and Florence would be free.

DUKE

Well, Strozzi—do you think I am afraid?

LUISA

No, milord, no. Everyone knows you are brave—Be as good as you are courageous.

STROZZI

Silence, child! I think you are begging this man,

(The Duke puts away his dagger in its sheathe and picks up his sword.)

LUISA

(in a low voice)

Father, father—let me—God will give strength to my words—

(bowing to the Duke)

Milord—

FRA LEONARDO

(raising her)

Rise, child! There's no treating between innocence and crime! No pact between an angel and a demon—Rise.

DUKE

You are wrong, monk—she is so beautiful that, I was going to forget the offense so as only to remember my love.

STROZZI

(Enveloping Luisa in his arms)

My child! My child!

FRA LEONARDO

O my God, my God! If you see such things without thunder, I will say that your mercy is greater than your justice.

DUKE

You see—I left to God the time to strike

(calling)

Jacopo—Hungarian.

(The Hungarian and Jacopo enter.)

HUNGARIAN

At your orders. Highness.

DUKE

(pointing to Fra Leonardo and Strozzi)

Put these two men in the hands of the guards.

LUISA

Milord! Milord! In the name of heaven, don't separate father from daughter: Don't tear the priest from his god.

STROZZI

Shut up and stay here. Not a word more—not a step forward—or I will curse you.

LUISA

Oh!

(she falls on her knees at the prie-dieu)

STROZZI

Goodbye, my child! The Lord alone will watch over you from now on—But never forget that it is Lorenzino who kills me!

LUISA

(extending her arms towards him)

Father! Father!

(to Duke)

Oh milord—is their nothing I can do to save my father?

DUKE

(returning to her)

Indeed there is, child! For you alone can do something

to save him.

LUISA

What must I do. Milord?

DUKE

Lorenzino will tell you.

(He leaves)

LUISA

(in despair)

Oh! My God! Everyone accuses him—Even the Duke.

LORENZINO

(enters through the side door then, resting a hand on Luisa's shoulder—shows her the crucifix)

This will justify him!

(CURTAIN)

ACT IV

A room with old half effaced frescoes—in the prison of Barghello. In the foreground at each side two columns which sustain the vault.

Fra Leonardo, leaning against a column, is talking with Strozzi. Selvaggio Aldobrandini is lying on a bench. Bernardo Corsini and Vittorio dei Pazzi are also prisoners.

Bernardo Corsini is mounted on a stool, busily engraving his name on the mural with a nail. Vittorio, standing near him, watches him do it.

FRA LEONARDO

(turning in their direction)

What are you doing, Bernardo?

BERNARDO

You can see. Father. I am writing my unworthy name near those of the martyrs who preceded me down here and who await me in heaven.

(He comes down and gives the nail to Vittorio.)

VITTORIO

My turn! By the Christ, these walls will one day be The Golden Book of Florence. Wait, here's the name of Jacob dei Pazzi my ancestor. Hers's that of Jerome Savonarola—Here's that of Nicolas Carducci—Here's one of Dante de Castiglione—Long Live God—what a beautiful guard of noble ghosts for liberty, exiled from earth—must be on high.

SELVAGGIO

Scratch in my name, too Pazzi. Posterity must know that I was one of those who didn't wish to live in slavery. And if the wall is too hard, come take my blood to write my name instead of carving it—my wound is still fresh and won't refuse you. Write—Selvaggio Aldobrandini died for liberty.

VITTORIO

Your turn, Strozzi.

(passing the nail to Strozzi)

STROZZI

(writing and repeating what he writes)

God protect me from those I trust. And I will protect myself from those I distrust.

VITTORIO

A beautiful maxim—but expressed on the walls of a prison it has the defect of arriving a little too late.

(The other prisoners write their name. The door at the rear opens.)

A FAMILIAR OF THE INQUISITION

(entering)

Is Filippo Strozzi returned from interrogation?

STROZZI

Yes—who asks for him?

Familiar

A young girl who has leave to spend a half hour with him.

STROZZI

A young girl?—It can't be Luisa.

LUISA

(from the door)

It's me, papa.

STROZZI

Come, my child. I have pardoned you; the others will pardon you, I hope.

(Luisa comes forward. The familiar leaves.)

Oh my child—

(terrified)

Whose permission do you have to see me?

LUISA

From the Duke himself.

STROZZI

How did you get it from him?

LUISA

I went to get it.

STROZZI

Where?

LUISA

At the palace.

STROZZI

At the palace. The Duke's palace? You've been to that infamous man?—To the bastard of the Medicis? Oh! I would have preferred never to see you again than to see you in this condition.

(he pushes her away)

FRA LEONARDO

(The young girl in his arms.)

Strozzi—be a man!

STROZZI

(without listening)

She's been to him—she went into that cavern of debauchery, into that den of lust, and how many years of your innocence have you paid to obtain permission to see me for a half hour? Answer, Luisa, answer!

LUISA

Father, God knows I don't deserve what you are saying to me. Anyway, I wasn't alone—It was Lorenzo who escorted me to the Duke's—and Lorenzo didn't leave me.

STROZZI

So then Luisa—There was no infamous condition?

LUISA

None, father, none—on the honor of the family! I threw myself at his feet, I asked to see you. The Duke and Lorenzo exchanged some words in low voices—then the Duke secured a pass and gave it to me—and I left without having had to blush for anything except the way he looked at me.

STROZZI

No matter. Under this clemency there is some terrible mystery. But, since a half hour only is given—let's put to profit the moments we have to spend together;—they are probably our last!

LUISA

Father!

STROZZI

I hope that God, in giving you the misfortune has given you the strength to bear it; in that case I can speak to you like a woman, and no longer like a child.

LUISA

Father, you make me tremble.

STROZZI

You know the man who asks for my head, you know the court which is judging me.

LUISA

Will you be condemned, father?

STROZZI

No, not yet, but I am going to be. Answer me as if I already was. Think that it's the peace of my last living hours that I am asking of you, think that the condemned not only must die, but he must die as a Christian, without cursing and without blaspheming.

FRA LEONARDO

Thanks to you, my God, who have brought this angel to bring him back the faith he had almost lost.

STROZZI

(in a solemn voice)

Luisa when you see my scaffold erected, when you know I am on my way to be sacrificed—swear to me you will have no part between your innocence and the infamy of this man, for by the soul of your mother, by my infinite love, Luisa, I declare that you won't save me—That I will die in despair—and that having lost me on earth, poor child, you won't recover me in heaven.

LUISA

(falling to her knees)

Father, I swear it to you. And let God punish me if I break my oath.

STROZZI

(placing his two hands on the head of his daughter and looking tenderly on her)

That's not all yet. The danger which pursues you during my agony may continue after my death. What the Duke is unable to obtain by terror he may try to obtain by violence.

LUISA

Father—

STROZZI

He can do anything; he does everything—He's infamous!

LUISA

My God—!

STROZZI

Luisa—you would much prefer to die young and pure, wouldn't you, than to live in shame and dishonor?

LUISA

Oh—yes, a hundred times yes, a thousand times yes. God is my witness.

STROZZI

Well—if ever you were to fall into the hands of that man—if you cannot see anyway to escape him, if even the mercy God, offers you no chance to hope——

LUISA

Finish father! Speak! Speak!

STROZZI

Well—a sole treasure remains with me which I hid from all eyes, a last consolation, a supreme friend which would spare me torture and the scaffold.—It's this poison—

LUISA

(seeing the little flash)

Give me, give me, father.

STROZZI

Good, good, Luisa! Thanks—This flask is freedom, it is honor; take it, Luisa—I give it to you. Remember that you are the daughter of Strozzi.

LUISA

It will be as you wish it, father, I swear it.

STROZZI

Now, I shall die in peace—And you, my God, who hear this oath—You will let it be accomplished,—won't you?

FAMILIAR

(entering with a masked man)

The half hour granted by the pass has expired—you must follow me.

LUISA

Oh! Already! Already!

STROZZI

Go, my daughter, and be blessed.

LUISA

Yet another moment! Yet another second!

STROZZI

No—go my child. Goodbye! No mercy from that man.

LUISA

Goodbye, father.

FRA LEONARDO

To meet again in heaven.

STROZZI

Yes, yes—

THE MASKED MAN

(low to Luisa as she passed near him)

Luisa!

LUISA

(shaking)

Lorenzo.

LORENZINO

You still have faith in me?

LUISA

More than ever!

LORENZINO

Well—till tonight.

LUISA

Till tonight!

(She leaves with the Familiar. Lorenzino still masked remains in the midst of the prisoners.)

VITTORIO

(to Lorenzino)

Who are you, who come amongst as masked? What spy of Morizio, what bailiff of the Duke's?

BERNARDO

Are you the torturer? We are ready for torture.

SELVAGGIO

Are you the executioner? We are ready for death.

VITTORIO

Look here, speak harbinger of evil. What news do you bring?

LORENZINO

I bring you the news that you are condemned to death and that you will all be executed tomorrow morning at break of day.

(Removing his mask.)

ALL

Lorenzino!

VITTORIO

What do you want?

BERNARDO

What do you seek?

LORENZINO

What does it matter to you who have nothing more to do in this world except to pray and to die?

FRA LEONARDO

Lorenzino! Have you descended into the catacombs to insult martyrs? What have you come to do here?

LORENZINO

You are going to know, because it's you I've come to see.

FRA LEONARDO

What do you want from me?

LORENZINO

Tell all these men to move away and to leave us isolated as much as possible.

FRA LEONARDO

Why's that?

LORENZINO

Because I have a secret to reveal to you, and because I too am in danger of death. I want you to hear my confession.

FRA LEONARDO

Your confession?

LORENZINO

Yes.

FRA LEONARDO

Me—hear your confession? And why me rather than someone else?

LORENZINO

Since when has the penitent lost the right to choose his confessor?

FRA LEONARDO

(to the prisoners)

Brothers—get back—all of you.

(sits down)

I am waiting.

LORENZINO

(kneeling before him)

Father, It's a year since I returned from Rome, already having in my heart the plan which I am going to execute today. Hardly returning to Florence, as I feared to share with others the feelings I had in me, I went about the different sections of the city, I questioned the houses of the poor, and the palaces of the rich—I mixed with the humble artisans and with the proud rich. A single voice like an immense wailing rose from all sides, accusing Duke Alexander. One wanted his money back, the other his honor, another a son. All wept, all lamented, all accused, and I said to myself—"No, it's not just that an entire people should suffer from the tyranny of a single man."

FRA LEONARDO

Ah! What we had dreamed was really true?

LORENZINO

Then I cast my eyes about me, I saw shame on all faces, fear in all hearts, corruption in all souls! I looked about for what I could lean on, and I felt that the weight of terror caused everything to collapse in my hand. The Secret Accusation was everywhere—within and without; it penetrated families, it coursed through public places, it sat by the marital hearth, it rose on the milestones of the crossroads. I understood that whoever wished to conspire, in such times, could take no other confidant than his own thoughts, no other accomplice but his own arm; I understood that, like the first Brutus—that one must cover his face with a veil thick enough so no one could recognize him. Lorenzo became Lorenzino.

FRA LEONARDO

Continue! Continue!

LORENZINO

In order to get to the Duke, I had to distrust everyone—to trust only in myself. I became his courtier, his valet, his buffoon—I not only obeyed his orders, I even foresaw his desires. I anticipated his whims. In the course of a year Florence called me coward, traitor, infamous. For a year the scorn of my fellow citizens weighed on me—more heavily than the stone of a tomb. For a year all hearts distrusted me—except for a single one which, at last moment, perhaps will doubt—But still I've succeeded, finally. I've attained the end, which I wished to attain—Finally I've arrived at the end of my long and guilty route. This evening, I will deliver Florence—Tonight I will restore the liberty of my country. Tonight I will kill Duke Alexander.

FRA LEONARDO

Speak low! Speak low!

LORENZINO

But the Duke is clever, the Duke is strong—The Duke is brave: In trying to save Florence I may succumb in my turn. I need supreme absolution. Give it to me father—give it to me without hesitation, go—I've suffered enough on this earth that you cannot grudge me Heaven.

FRA LEONARDO

Lorenzino, it's a crime to absolve you, I know it—but I take this crime on myself and when God calls you to ask you to give and account for the blood you have spilled, I will present myself in your place saying, "Lord—don't look for the guilty—Lord the guilty one is before you!"

LORENZINO

Fine—all is said. No—he too like you, is condemned—and it is only a matter of time. When tomorrow they come to take you to the scaffold—cry out "Duke Alexander is dead! The Duke Alexander was murdered by Lorenzino! Open the house of Lorenzino—and you will find his body—" And the executioner himself will tremble, and the people will run to my house in the via Largha—and the people will find the body of the Duke and instead of being taken to the scaffold you will be carried in triumph!

FRA LEONARDO

And you?

LORENZINO

It will be I who opens the room where the Duke's body will be—to the people. Goodbye father.

(turning towards the prisoners grouped at the back)

Place—gentlemen.

VITTORIO

And if we don't wish to let you pass?

BERNARDO

And if we wish to revenge ourselves before we die?

STROZZI

If we've decided to choke you with our bare hands?

ALL

Let him die—The man who betrayed us all! Let the traitor die—Let the infamous one die.

(Lorenzino puts his sword in his hand as if to open a passageway.)

FRA LEONARDO

(rushing between him and the prisoners)

Brothers, let this man pass—and bow to him—He's the greatest of us all!

(CURTAIN)

ACT V

Lorenzino's room. Large door in the rear. To the right front—a door opening on a stairway—on the same side towards the rear—another door—between the two doors—a window. To the left, the entry to a small oratory the interior of which can be seen—further back a door giving on a cabinet.

LORENZINO

Return to your home, milord, do the honor of supper to your guests, drink two cups rather than one—In a half hour Luisa will be here.

DUKE

I can count on it?

LORENZINO

When I promise you! Have I ever promised you a thing that I did not managed?

DUKE

Then in a half an hour.

LORENZINO

Yes—Only I don't wish to leave the house. I have no one I can trust. You are sure of the Hungarian.

DUKE

As myself.

LORENZINO

Lend him to me to go find our beauty in distress.

DUKE

Nice—she'll know he belongs to me and she won't follow him.

LORENZINO

With a letter from me which promises her the life of her father she will follow the devil to Hell! Besides, it's not the first time the child has come here. Isn't she my fiancee?

DUKE

Then why all these precautions?

LORENZINO

To save appearances, for God's sake.

DUKE

Then take the Hungarian: I put him at your disposition.

LORENZINO

Call him and tell him he must obey me in all particulars.

DUKE

(opening the door in the rear)

Come here, and, on your head, do whatever Lorenzino orders you.

(The Hungarian enters)

LORENZINO

(writing)

Oh—by God—its very simple!

(to the Hungarian)

You are going to go to the Old Plaza Saint Maria—to the house of the young girl of the holy basin—you will give her this letter, she will follow you, and you will bring her here. Here's the key to the street door.

HUNGARIAN

And after she gets here?

LORENZINO

You will go inform His Highness.

HUNGARIAN

It will be done as milord desires.

DUKE

Go and return quickly.

(The Hungarian leaves and the Duke prepares to go himself.)

LORENZINO

Milord, your word that none of your guests will know where you are going nor why you left the table?

DUKE

I give it to you.

LORENZINO

Now, your word that you won't forget that you have given it to me!

DUKE

My precious!

LORENZINO

Let's not get angry. I prefer two promises to one. On your word as a gentleman?

DUKE

On my word as a gentleman.

LORENZINO

Then everything will be fine.

DUKE

What's the matter with you?

LORENZINO

Me?

DUKE

You're as pale as death and now sweat is running down

you face!

LORENZINO

Your Highness is very good—it's nothing—So! Milord—go!

DUKE

In a half hour!

LORENZINO

Sooner, if I can manage.

(The Duke leaves. Lorenzino goes to the window and looks down the street.)

LORENZINO

The cold air does me some good! Michel should be at his post—! A man is walking in the street—It's probably he—Psst—! It's him!

MICHEL

(in the street)

Milord?

LORENZINO

Here's the key, come in and come up to the second floor—you know the way. Hey!

(He throws him the key and then goes to look at himself in a mirror)

His Highness was right. I have a pale face—But my heart is firm.

MICHEL

(entering)

Here I am, milord.

LORENZINO

I am happy to find you so exact at the rendezvous. Are you ready?

MICHEL

Is it for tonight?

LORENZINO

In an hour everything will be finished.

MICHEL

Where's it going to be?

LORENZINO

You don't have to leave.

MICHEL

The thing will happen in your home?

LORENZINO

Even here.

MICHEL

But aren't you afraid that someone will hear—even at the Duke's—shouting and the clash of arms.

LORENZINO

For a year now, the neighbors have heard so many shouts and clashes of the sword—they won't pay attention, don't worry.

MICHEL

Your Excellency has not forgotten that he made me a promise.

LORENZINO

Recall it to me.

MICHEL

It's that, once you are avenged—I will be free to avenge myself in my turn.

LORENZINO

You intend to kill the Duke.

MICHEL

More than ever.

LORENZINO

And neither god, nor money nor threats, nor prayers will make you renounce your project?

MICHEL

I have sworn an oath to kill him without pity, without mercy.

LORENZINO

Then what you told me is really true?

MICHEL

I told you the complete truth.

LORENZINO

But it's impossible to believe.

MICHEL

Why's that?

LORENZINO

No man is capable of such cruelty.

MICHEL

Duke Alexander is not a man.

LORENZINO

She was beautiful, this young girl?

MICHEL

Beautiful like an angel.

LORENZINO

I have forgotten her name.

MICHEL

Nella.

LORENZINO

And dead?

MICHEL

Dead!

LORENZINO

How old?

MICHEL

Eighteen.

LORENZINO

That's very young.

MICHEL

It's too old, since for two years misfortune and shame had come into her life.

LORENZINO

And you say, that after having given you hope to be her husband—Duke Alexander—?

MICHEL

Oh—Let me alone, milord! Don't you understand that at each word you speak rage mounts to my head and gives me vertigo—Be silent, you will render me senseless—It's not a question of me, it's about you—it's you who are going to be avenged, right? And not me—I am obliged to purchase my vengeance with the life of a man other than the one who offended me—Tell me who is this man who is sufficiently abandoned to serve as the shield of the Duke—Name this man—tell me his name! I am ready.

LORENZINO

I have no need to tell you his name—you will see him.

MICHEL

Why, do I know him?

LORENZINO

You have a bad memory Michel! You named four men to me who were with the Duke on that fatal night—and I've told you that the one on whom I have to avenge myself was one of those men.

MICHEL

It's time, that suffices.

(seeing Lorenzino listening)

Someone is shutting the street door. Is that him?

LORENZINO

No—not yet—But it is someone who must not see you.

(pointing to the left)

Go into that room and don't leave until I call you to my aid. Think of the Duke—dream of your vengeance and then, when I have need of you—let me find you sword in hand—Go in!

(pushing him into the room)

HUNGARIAN

(to Luisa who follows him)

There! Now, Signorina, do you still suspect?

LORENZINO

Luisa!

LUISA

Lorenzo!

LORENZINO

(to Hungarian)

You know what remains to be done?

HUNGARIAN

Yes milord.

LORENZINO

Give me the key—You will close the door behind you—

(tossing him a purse)

Here!

HUNGARIAN

(aside)

Decidedly, I will never understand anything about this man.

(The Hungarian leaves)

(Lorenzino gestures to Luisa to remain quiet, listens to the steps of the Hungarian who goes off after having shut the street door.)

LORENZINO

You didn't doubt me Luisa—Thanks!

LUISA

My Lorenzo—The hour that I suspect you will be the hour of my death.

LORENZINO

(going to the door at the rear)

Wait, while I shut this door.

(Luisa follows him with her eyes—he shuts the door and returns to the young girl.)

Now—listen to me.

LUISA

As one listens to the voice of god—But, before all—my father.

LORENZINO

(in an abrupt voice)

I told you that your father would be saved, and he will be. But that's not enough. In thinking about him, I thought of us—my beloved. In an hour we will leave

Florence.

LUISA

Where are we going?

LORENZINO

To Venice. I have there a license given me by the Bishop of Mozze to take post horses. Once free—your father will rejoin you.

LUISA

Then, let us leave, my Lorenzo.

LORENZINO

(in a voice which is changing—more and more)

No—not yet! Before we can leave a great event must be accomplished, Luisa.

LUISA

Where's that?

LORENZINO

Here.

LUISA

What do you mean, here?

LORENZINO

(pointing to the room to the right)

Here in this room.

LUISA

But me, me?

LORENZINO

You, Luisa, you will be in this oratory where you will pray for me—Whatever you hear, whatever quarrel there is, whatever action takes place—you will not budge, you won't move at all, you won't utter a word—When everything is over, I will open it for you, you will shut your eyes as you cross this room and—we will leave.

LUISA

Lorenzo! Lorenzo! You make me shudder!

LORENZINO

Hush! Don't you hear?

LUISA

Steps in the corridor.

LORENZINO

That's right. Go into this oratory, Luisa here's the supreme moment: call all your courage to your aid—and, and if you see death enter—(pushing her into the oratory, a finger to her lips) Be silent!

LUISA

Holy Mother of Angels—What's going to happen?

LORENZINO

Pray!

(He shuts the door of the oratory and puts the key in his pocket. The door at the back opens. Luisa is on her knees in the oratory praying.)

DUKE

(entering)

Come, Lorenzino, I recognize that you are a man of your word.

LUISA

The Duke's voice.

LORENZINO

The Hungarian told Your Highness?

DUKE

That thinking she was following the shepherd the sweet lamb followed the butcher!

LUISA

(rising to one knee)

What's he saying?

LORENZINO

(pointing to the oratory)

Hush—there!

DUKE

Why there and not here?

LORENZINO

I know the way you are at table, I didn't know how many cups you counted on emptying—if you were drunk, I didn't want you to frighten her.

LUISA

My God, my God—did I really understand?

DUKE

You see, I have taken care of myself.

LORENZINO

Yes, your Highness is completely presentable

(escorting him to the room at the right)

So, milord—

DUKE

Where are you leading me to?

LORENZINO

To my own, room, by God—In five minutes I will hand her over to you.

LUISA

Ah!

(she opens the window as if to throw herself out)

Bars! Bars!

LORENZINO

Once in this room, I slam the door behind her—The rest is your concern—

LUISA

Oh! He! Himself—The poison! The poison! Thanks, father.

(she empties the flask in a gulp and falls on her knees on the prie-dieu)

LORENZINO

(entering the room behind the Duke, but still within view of the audience)

Aren't you going to get rid of your dressing gown and your sword?

DUKE

(in the room)

Of my dressing gown, yes—as for my sword it never leaves my side except to sleep by my pillow.

LORENZINO

You are a man of prudence, milord.

DUKE

And that precaution wasn't misplaced at the Marchessa de Cibo's.

(At that moment, both enter the room Michel leaves his hiding place sword in hand, listening.)

MICHEL

God forgive me—it's the Duke's voice.

DUKE

(out of sight, uttering a shout)

Ah—traitor!

LORENZINO

Die, wretch! Die infamous one! Help, Michel!

DUKE

Oh—I won't die from a knife wound—

(He rushes on stage, and finds himself face to face—with Michel who runs him through with his sword.)

MICHEL

No—but you are going to die of a sword stroke.

DUKE

Michel!

MICHEL

(pushing him back in the room)

Remember Nella!

DUKE

(out of sight)

I am dead—

(The sound of a body collapsing can be heard.)

LUISA

Luisa—Holy Madonna—They are killing—killing—

(Lorenzino rushes out of the room all bloody wounded in his hand and cheek.)

LORENZINO

Luisa! Come! Come!

(Opening the door of the oratory)

LUISA

Ah! Wretch, I understand.

LORENZINO

Let's not lose an instant, my love, my life—. Come! Come! What's the matter with you? Why do you hesitate? He's dead! Florence is free and your father is saved.

LUISA

(unable to walk and resting on her arm)

Forgive me, my beloved Lorenzo—but I doubted you—and I told you that the moment I were to doubt you would be the moment of my death—

LORENZINO

Well?

LUISA

My father gave me—in case I were to fall into the Duke's hands—This flask of poison—Not only did I think I'd fallen into his hands but worse still, I thought it was you who had delivered me to him!

LORENZINO

And then? Speak—will you speak!

LUISA

(showing him the flask)

Look!

LORENZINO

The flask is empty—Oh, misfortune on me—I am cursed!

LUISA

Lorenzo, my Lorenzo.

LORENZINO

Luisa.

LUISA

Oh—in your arms! Against your heart.

LORENZINO

(weeping)

My God! My God!

(Luisa slides to her knees)

Help! Help! She's dying.

(Luisa utters a long sigh)

Dead!

(Despairing silence during which Michel appears in the door of the room)

I had only two loves—Florence and Luisa—I have only one religion: Liberty!

(CURTAIN)

ABOUT THE AUTHOR

Frank J. Morlock has written and translated many plays since retiring from the legal profession in 1992. His translations have also appeared on Project Gutenberg, the Alexandre Dumas Père web page, Literature in the Age of Napoléon, Infinite Artistries.com, and Munsey's (formerly Blackmask). In 2006 he received an award from the North American Jules Verne Society for his translations of Verne's plays. He lives and works in México.

www.ingramcontent.com/pod-product-compliance
Lightning Source LLC
LaVergne TN
LVHW041542070426
835507LV00011B/885